REH ☆ PRO LESSONS

ARTFUL ARPEGGIOS

by
Don Mock

ISBN 978-0-634-02261-6

HAL•LEONARD®

Visit Hal Leonard Online at
www.halleonard.com

Contact us:
Hal Leonard
7777 West Bluemound Road
Milwaukee, WI 53213
Email: info@halleonard.com

In Europe, contact:
Hal Leonard Europe Limited
42 Wigmore Street
Marylebone, London, W1U 2RN
Email: info@halleonardeurope.com

In Australia, contact:
Hal Leonard Australia Pty. Ltd.
4 Lentara Court
Cheltenham, Victoria, 3192 Australia
Email: info@halleonard.com.au

Introduction

The definition of an arpeggio is the notes of a chord played in succession rather than simultaneously. Each chord has an inherent arpeggio, but learning arpeggio fingerings for every chord would be laborious and impractical. However, you can deceive the listener into hearing virtually any chordal sound you desire by playing a basic arpeggio utilizing substitution principles.

Hopefully, this book can offer you some effective ways to melodically create any chordal sound you desire. These arpeggio concepts, in conjunction with scales, intervals, and rhythmic variations, should offer some fruitful musical ideas. Be patient with any technical problems you may encounter, as time and practice will prove beneficial. To further enhance your knowledge and use of arpeggios, listen to your favorite players and study how they use them.

Don Mock, circa 1977

About the Author

Guitarist Don Mock grew up in the Pacific Northwest on rock and blues. Early in his career, he broadened his music interests to include jazz.. Don began his teaching career in 1972 at the Cornish School of the Allied Arts and Olympic Jr. College, both in Washington State. In 1974, he began to manage teaching seminars in the Northwest for guitar legend Howard Roberts. Three years later, Roberts brought Don to Los Angeles to help start the Guitar Institute of Technology (G.I.T.). Don became a primary instructor and curriculum author for the school, and soon teamed up with publisher Roger E. Hutchinson to write and produce guitar method books for R.E.H. Publications. Don taught full-time at G.I.T. until 1983, and then began a part-time arrangement while commuting back and forth between Los Angeles and Seattle. He also traveled around the United States and Europe, giving seminars to promote G.I.T. with Howard Roberts, Robben Ford, Keith Wyatt, and Tommy Tedesco. In the late '80s and early '90s, Don focused on directing and producing videos for G.I.T. (now with its parent name, Musicians Institute) and R.E.H. Publications. During this time, he worked on video projects with a virtual "who's who" of guitar, including Joe Pass, Alan Holdsworth, Paul Gilbert, Steve Morse, and Al Di Meola. As a recording artist, Don has appeared as a sideman on several albums and has two solo efforts: *Mock One* and *Speed of Light*. He is also a lifelong fan of unlimited hydroplane racing and has produced and written scores for several boat racing video productions. Don currently heads up the Hydroplane and Raceboat Museums video productions, adding his unique compositions and guitar talents to the programs.

Table of Contents

NOTE: Use track **79** to tune up.

Geometrical Location of Intervals

By definition, an interval is the distance between any two notes. The next page will serve as a quick visual guide for the geometrical location of intervals on the guitar. This information is vital; it is the foundation on which the concept of this book is built. Throughout the book, we will be playing arpeggios that begin a certain distance (interval) from the root of the original chord.

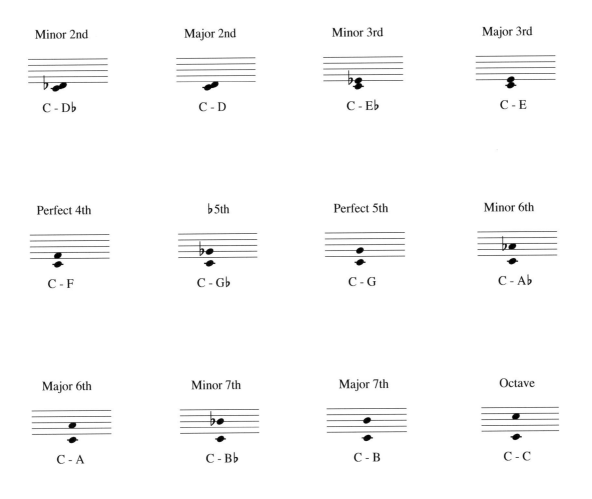

Try this quiz. If you need help, refer to the next page.

Starting on low G, sixth string third fret, go up a major 3rd (B); up a 4th (E); down a major 7th (low F); up a 5th; up a minor 2nd; down a major 3rd; up an octave; down a ♭5th; up a major 3rd; down a major 6th; up a major 7th; up an octave; up a ♭5th; down a 4th; down a minor 6th; down a ♭5th; down a 4th; up a major 2nd. You should now be on F.

Geometrical Location of Intervals

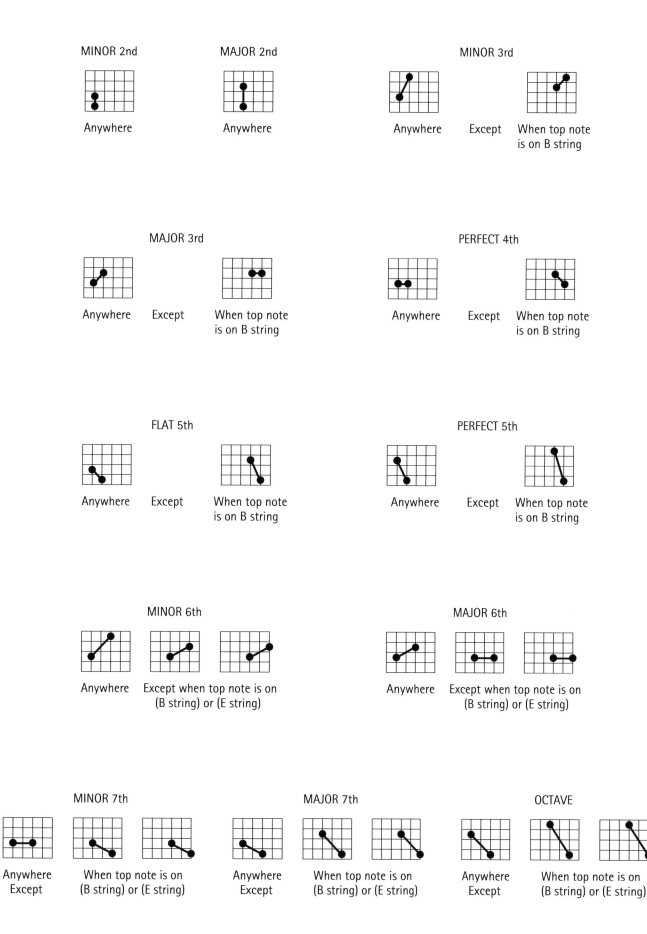

Harmonized Major Scale

If you understand where chords originate and learn arpeggios for each chord type, you will be prepared to apply the substitution rules discussed later in this book. So let's look at the three most commonly used scales.

C MAJOR SCALE

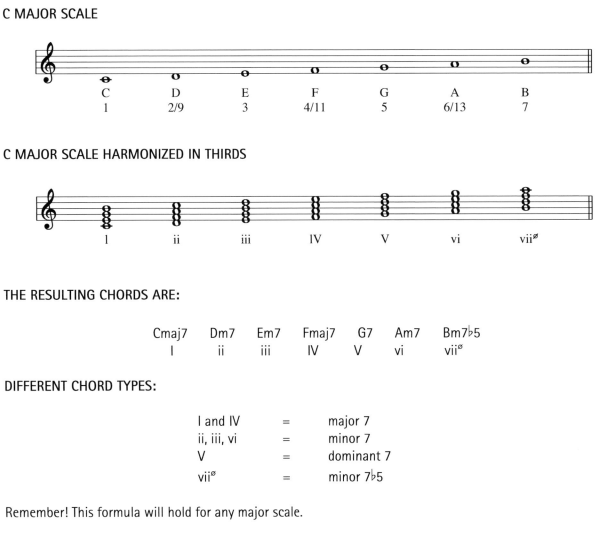

C	D	E	F	G	A	B
1	2/9	3	4/11	5	6/13	7

C MAJOR SCALE HARMONIZED IN THIRDS

I	ii	iii	IV	V	vi	vii^ø

THE RESULTING CHORDS ARE:

Cmaj7	Dm7	Em7	Fmaj7	G7	Am7	Bm7♭5
I	ii	iii	IV	V	vi	vii^ø

DIFFERENT CHORD TYPES:

I and IV	=	major 7
ii, iii, vi	=	minor 7
V	=	dominant 7
vii^ø	=	minor 7♭5

Remember! This formula will hold for any major scale.

So we need four kinds of arpeggios to accommodate chords resulting from a harmonized major scale:

major 7
minor 7
dominant 7
minor 7♭5

Arpeggio Fingerings

The arpeggio fingerings in this book are practical and commonly used, but are not the only possibilities. The serious guitarist should explore the guitar neck for any and all alternate fingerings.

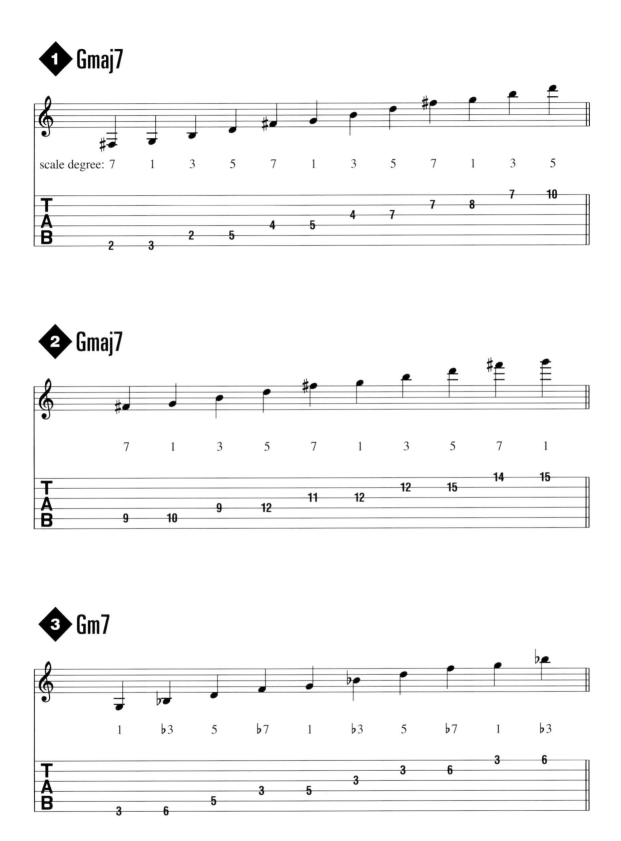

Gm7

 Cm7

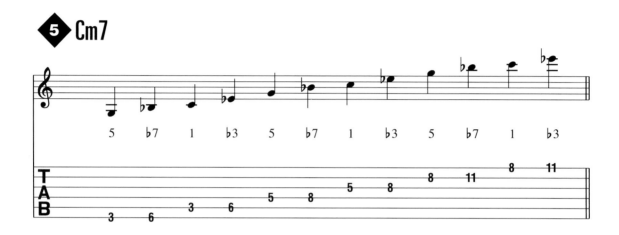

6 **G7**

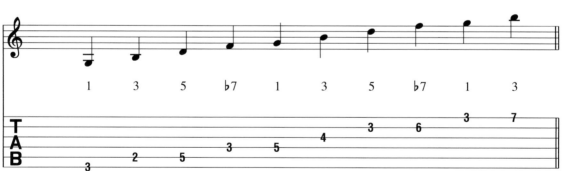

7 G7

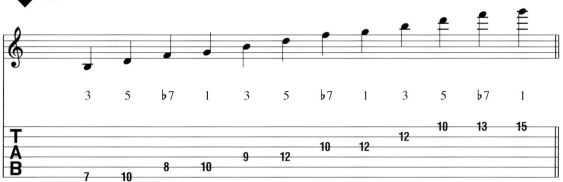

8 Dm7♭5

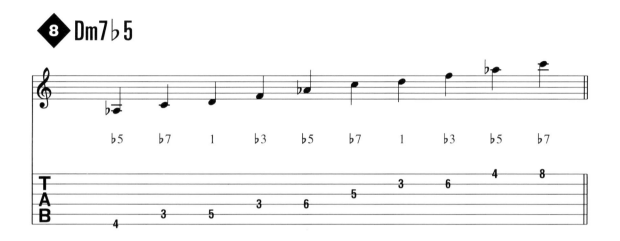

9 Dm7♭5

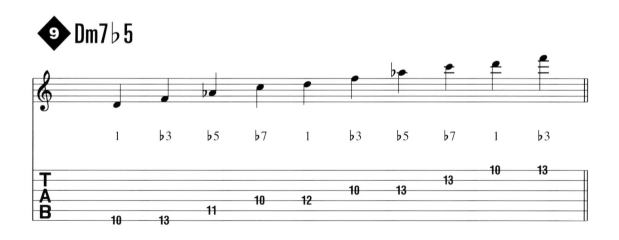

Harmonized Jazz Melodic Minor Scale

C JAZZ MELODIC MINOR SCALE

C D Eb F G A B

HARMONIZED C JAZZ MELODIC MINOR SCALE

i ii III+ IV V vi⌀ vii⌀

THE RESULTING CHORDS ARE:

Cm(maj7)	Dm7	Ebmaj7#5	F7	G7	Am7b5	Bm7b5
i	ii	III+	IV	V	vi⌀	vii⌀

DIFFERENT CHORD TYPES:

i	=	minor-major 7
ii	=	minor 7
III+	=	major 7#5
IV and V	=	dominant 7
vi⌀ and vii⌀	=	minor 7b5

Remember! This formula will hold for any jazz melodic minor scale.

We are going to need two more arpeggios because two additional chord types (minor-major 7 and major 7#5) have resulted from the harmonization of this scale. The other chord types were already noted from harmonizing the major scale.

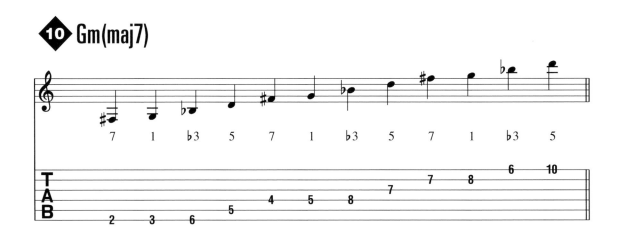

10 Gm(maj7)

Arpeggio Fingerings

11 Gm(maj7)

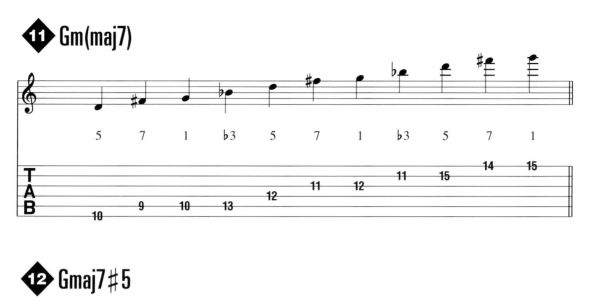

12 Gmaj7♯5

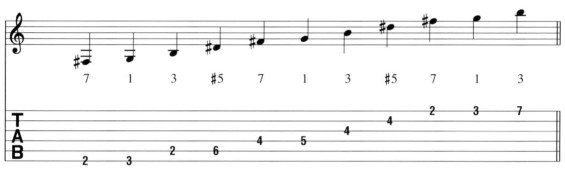

13 Gmaj7♯5

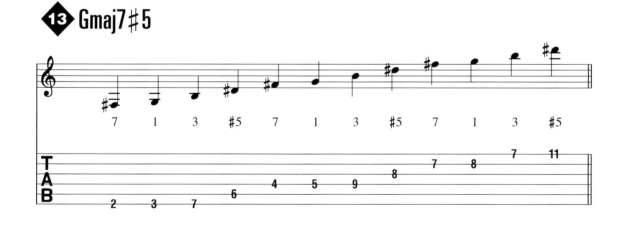

14 Cmaj7♯5

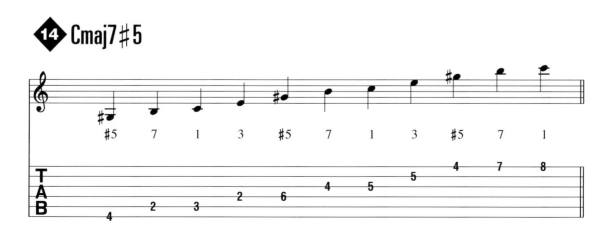

Harmonized Harmonic Minor Scale

C HARMONIC MINOR SCALE

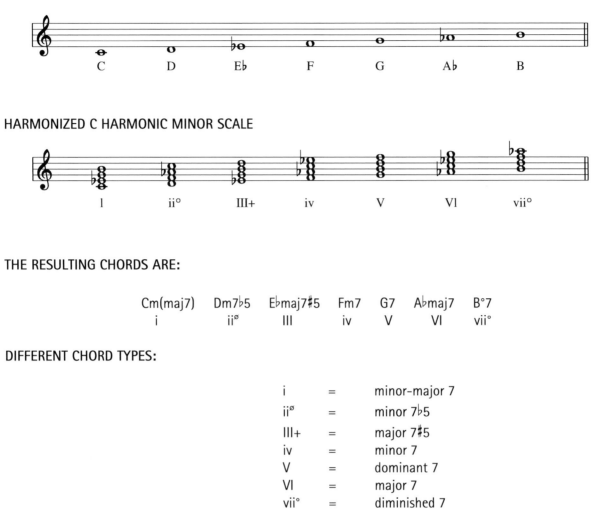

HARMONIZED C HARMONIC MINOR SCALE

THE RESULTING CHORDS ARE:

Cm(maj7)	Dm7♭5	E♭maj7♯5	Fm7	G7	A♭maj7	B°7
i	ii^ø	III	iv	V	VI	vii°

DIFFERENT CHORD TYPES:

i	=	minor-major 7
ii^ø	=	minor 7♭5
III+	=	major 7♯5
iv	=	minor 7
V	=	dominant 7
VI	=	major 7
vii°	=	diminished 7

Remember! This formula will hold for any harmonic minor scale.

Compared to the chord types that resulted from the harmonization of the other two scales, we now know we are going to need an arpeggio to accommodate the diminished 7 chord.

Arpeggio Fingerings

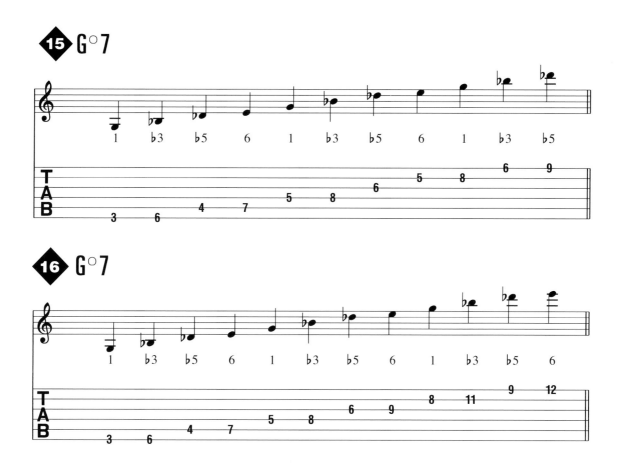

There are four additional arpeggios that you should become familiar with. They are major, minor, augmented, and major 7♭5 arpeggios.

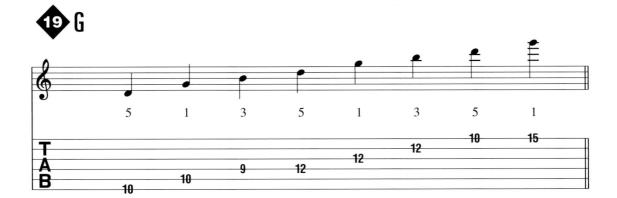

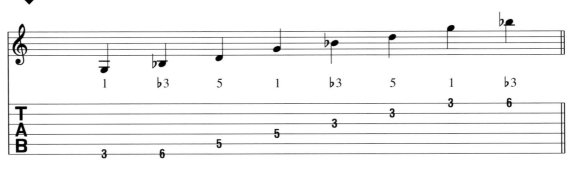

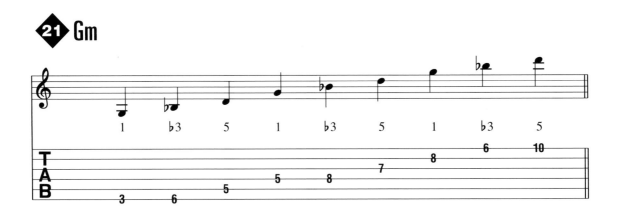

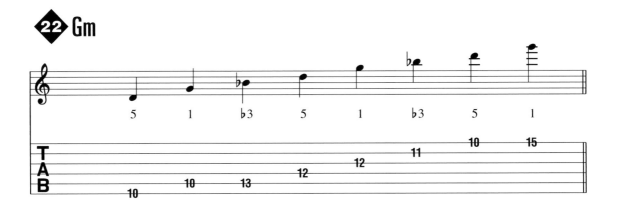

G+

24 **G+**

25 **Cmaj7♭5**

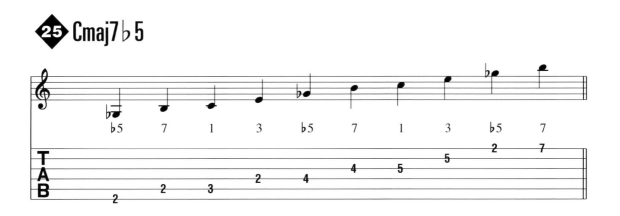

26 **Cmaj7♭5**

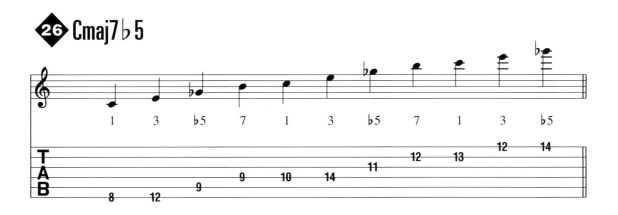

Creating Major Sounds

C MAJOR SCALE
(Ionian)

C	D	E	F	G	A	B
1	2/9	3	4/11	5	6/13	7

MAJOR 7 CONSTRUCTION

1(C)	3(E)	5(G)	7(B)

Here's where we start. Using the major chord family (the key of C is used in order to make all examples as explicit as possible), we are going to apply different arpeggios against the major 7 chord and see what other major chord sounds we can create. We will use the I, iii, and vi arpeggios in the key of C.

Created
Chordal Sound

Cmaj7 (I) arpeggio played against a Cmaj7 chord   =   Cmaj7
(C, E, G, B)   =   Notes of the Cmaj7 arpeggio
(1, 3, 5, 7)   =   Notes compared to a C chord

MAJOR 9 SUBSTITUTION RULE

Playing a minor 7 arpeggio up a major 3rd from the root of the major chord will create a major 9 sound. Why? It contains the D note, which is the 9th of C.

Em7 (iii) arpeggio played against a Cmaj7 chord   =   Cmaj9
(E, G, B, D)   =   Notes of the Em7 arpeggio
(3, 5, 7, 9)   =   Notes compared to a C chord

MAJOR 6 SUBSTITUTION RULE

Playing a minor 7 arpeggio down a minor 3rd from the root of the major chord will create a major 6 sound. Why? It contains the A note, which is the 6th of C.

Am7 (vi) arpeggio played against Cmaj7 chord   =   C6
(A, C, E, G)   =   Notes of the Am7 arpeggio
(6, 1, 3, 5)   =   Notes compared to a C chord

Major Sounds

This is an example of four bars of Cmaj7 utilizing the substitution principles we just learned.

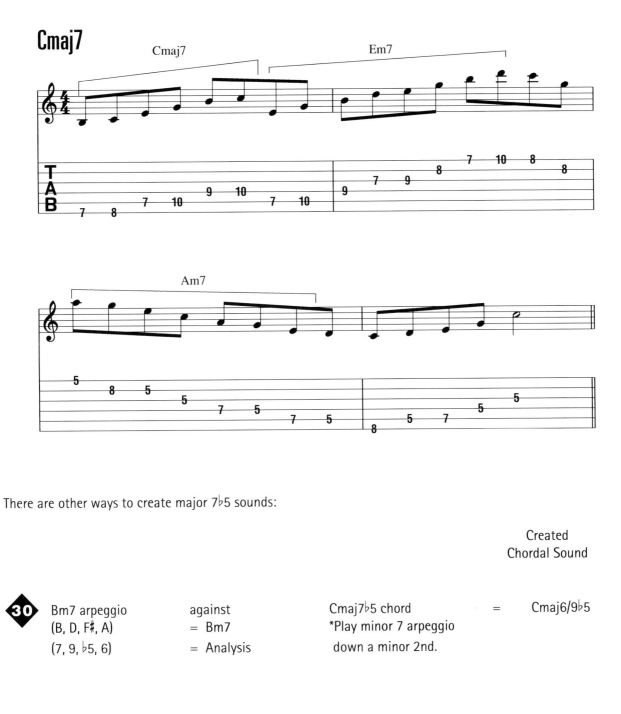

There are other ways to create major 7♭5 sounds:

				Created Chordal Sound
30 Bm7 arpeggio	against	Cmaj7♭5 chord	=	Cmaj6/9♭5
(B, D, F♯, A)	= Bm7	*Play minor 7 arpeggio		
(7, 9, ♭5, 6)	= Analysis	down a minor 2nd.		
31 G♭m7♭5 arpeggio	against	Cmaj7♭5 chord	=	Cmaj6♭5
(G♭, A, C, E)	= G♭m7♭5	*Play minor 7♭5 arpeggio		
(♭5, 6, 1, 3)	= Analysis	up a flat 5th.		

(Audio track **32** features D and G triads played over Cmaj7.)

* Substitution rule

Creating Minor Sounds

D MINOR 7 SCALE
(Dorian)

D	E	F	G	A	B	C
1	2/9	♭3	4/11	5	6/13	♭7

MINOR 7 CONSTRUCTION

1(D) ♭3(F) 5(A) ♭7(C)

Notice that we are using arpeggios of chords all resulting from a harmonized C major scale.
Dm7 = ii chord, key of C.

Created
Chordal Sound

33 Dm7 (ii) arpeggio   against   Dm7 chord   =   Dm7
(D, F, A, C)   = Dm7 arpeggio
(1, ♭3, 5, ♭7)   = Analysis

34 Fmaj7 (IV) arpeggio   against   Dm7 chord   =   Dm9
(F, A, C, E)   = Fmaj7   *Play major 7 arpeggio
(♭3, 5, ♭7, 9)   = Analysis   up a minor 3rd.

35 Am7 (vi) arpeggio   against   Dm7 chord   =   Dm11
(A, C, E, G)   = Am7   *Play minor 7 arpeggio
(5, ♭7, 9, 11)   = Analysis   up a 5th.

36 Bm7♭5 (vii°) arpeggio   against   Dm7 chord   =   Dm6
(B, D, F, A)   = Bm7♭5   *Play minor 7♭5 arpeggio
(6, 1, ♭3, 5)   = Analysis   down a minor 3rd.

37 Cmaj7 (I) arpeggio   against   Dm7 chord   =   Dm13
(C, E, G, B)   = Cmaj7   *Play major 7 arpeggio
(♭7, 9, 11, 13)   = Analysis   down a major 2nd.

38 G7 (V) arpeggio   against   Dm7 chord   =   Dm6(add11)
(G, B, D, F)   = G7   *Play dominant 7 arpeggio
(11, 6, 1, ♭3)   = Analysis   up a 4th.

39 Em7 (iii) arpeggio   against   Dm7 chord   =   Dm13
(E, G, B, D)   = Em7   *Play minor 7 arpeggio
(9, 11, 13, 1)   = Analysis   up a major 2nd.

(Audio track **40** features a discussion of the above arpeggios played over Dm7.)

* Substitution rule

18

Minor Sounds

Creating Minor 7♭5 Sounds

B MINOR 7♭5 SCALE
(Locrian)

B	C	D	E	F	G	A
1	♭2/♭9	♭3	4/11	♭5	6/13	♭7

MINOR 7♭5 CONSTRUCTION

1(B)   ♭3(D)   ♭5(F)   ♭7(A)

Created
Chordal Sound

41 Bm7♭5 arpeggio   against   Bm7♭5 chord   =   Bm7♭5
(B, D, F, A)   =   Bm7♭5
(1, ♭3, ♭5, ♭7)   =   Analysis

42 Dm7 arpeggio   against   Bm7♭5 chord   =   Bm7♭5♭9
(D, F, A, C)   =   Dm7   *Play minor 7 arpeggio
(♭3, ♭5, ♭7, ♭9)   =   Analysis   up a minor 3rd.

43 G7 arpeggio   against   Bm7♭5 chord   =   Bm13♭5
(G, B, D, F)   =   G7   *Play dominant 7 arpeggio
(13, 1, ♭3, ♭5)   =   Analysis   down a major 3rd.

44 B° arpeggio   against   Bm7♭5 chord   =   Bm6♭5
(B, D, F, A♭)   =   B°   *Play diminished arpeggio
(1, ♭3, ♭5, 6)   =   Analysis   on the root.

(Audio track **45** features Fmaj7 played over Bm7♭5.)

* Substitution rule

Creating Dominant Sounds

G DOMINANT SCALE
(Mixolydian)

G	A	B	C	D	E	F
1	2/9	3	4/11	5	6/13	♭7

DOMINANT 7 CONSTRUCTION

1(G)   3(B)   5(D)   ♭7(F)

Notice we are using arpeggios of chords all resulting from a harmonized C major scale.
G7 = V chord, key of C.

						Created Chordal Sound
46	G7 (V) arpeggio		against	G7 chord	=	G7
	(G, B, D, F)	=	G7 arpeggio			
	(1, 3, 5, ♭7)	=	Notes compared to a G7 chord			
47	Bm7♭5 (viiø) arpeggio		against	G7 chord	=	G9
	(B, D, F, A)	=	Bm7♭5	*Play minor 7♭5 arpeggio		
	(3, 5, ♭7, 9)	=	Analysis	up a major 3rd.		
48	Dm7 (ii) arpeggio		against	G7 chord	=	G11
	(D, F, A, C)	=	Dm7 arpeggio	*Play minor 7 arpeggio		
	(5, ♭7, 9, 11)	=	Analysis	up a 5th.		
49	Fmaj7 (IV) arpeggio		against	G7 chord	=	G13
	(F, A, C, E)	=	Fmaj7 arpeggio	*Play major 7 arpeggio		
	(♭7, 9, 11, 13)	=	Analysis	down a major 2nd.		

(Audio track **50** features Gm7 and Am7 played over G7.)

* Substitution rule

G7

Creating Altered Dominant Sounds

					Created Chordal Sound
51 Ab° arpeggio		against	G7 chord	=	G7b9
(Ab, B, D, F)	=	Ab°	*Play diminished arpeggio		
(b9, 3, 5, b7)	=	Analysis	up minor 2nd.		
52 G+ arpeggio		against	G7 chord	=	G7#5
(G, B, D#)	=	G+	*Play augmented arpeggio		
(1, 3, #5)	=	Analysis	on root.		
53 A+ arpeggio		against	G7 chord	=	G9#11
(C#, F)	=	A+	*Play augmented arpeggio		
(#11, b7)	=	Analysis	up a major 2nd.		
54 Gm7 arpeggio		against	G7 chord	=	G7#9
(G, Bb, D, F)	=	Gm7	*Play minor 7 arpeggio		
(1, #9, 5, b7)	=	Analysis	on root.		
55 Ebmaj7#5 arpeggio		against	G7 chord	=	G7b13
(Eb, G, B, D)	=	Ebmaj7#5	*Play major 7+5 arpeggio		
(b13, 1, 3, 5)	=	Analysis	up a minor 6th.		
56 Fm7b5 arpeggio		against	G7 chord	=	G7b9#5
(F, Ab, B, Eb)	=	Fm7b5	*Play minor 7b5 arpeggio		
(b7, b9, 3, #5)	=	Analysis	down a major 2nd.		
57 Abm(maj7) arpeggio		against	G7 chord	=	G7b13b9
(Eb, G)	=	Abm(maj7)	*Play minor-major7 arpeggio		
(b13, 1)	=	Analysis	up a minor 2nd.		
58 Db7 arpeggio		against	G7 chord	=	G7b5b9
(Db, F, Ab, B)	=	Db7	*Play dominant arpeggio		
(b5, b7, b9, 3)	=	Analysis	up a flat 5th.		
59 Cm(maj7) arpeggio		against	G7 chord	=	G11b13
(Eb, G, B)	=	Cm(maj7)	*Play minor-major7 arpeggio		
(b13, 1, 3)	=	Analysis	up a 4th.		
60 Dbm7b5 arpeggio		against	G7 chord	=	G13b5
(Db, E, G, B)	=	Dbm7b5	*Play minor 7b5 arpeggio		
(b5, 13, 1, 3)	=	Analysis	up a flat 5th.		

* Substitution rule

Creating Altered Dominant Sounds Using Major Arpeggios

			Created Chordal Sound

61   E Major arpeggio   against   G7 chord   =   G13$\flat$9

     (E, G$\sharp$, B)   =   E major   *Play a major arpeggio

     (13, $\flat$9, 3)   =   Analysis   up a major 6th.

62   A Major arpeggio   against   G7 chord   =   G13$\flat$5

     (A, C$\sharp$, E)   =   A major   *Play major arpeggio

     (9, $\flat$5, 13)   =   Analysis   up a major 2nd.

63   D$\flat$ Major arpeggio   against   G7 chord   =   G7$^{\flat 9}_{\flat 5}$

     (D$\flat$, F, A$\flat$)   =   D$\flat$ major   *Play major arpeggio

     ($\flat$5, $\flat$7, $\flat$9)   =   Analysis   up a flat 5th.

64   B$\flat$ Major arpeggio   against   G7 chord   =   G7$\sharp$9

     (B$\flat$, D, F)   =   B$\flat$ major   *Play major arpeggio

     ($\sharp$9, 5, $\flat$7)   =   Analysis   up a minor 3rd.

* Substitution rule

Bi-Tonal Arpeggios

The idea here is to combine two arpeggios (bi-tonality) to create the desired chordal sound. In these examples, note the lower arpeggio is dominant and the higher arpeggio is major.

G7 arpeggio	plus	A major arpeggio	=	G13♭5
(G, B, D, F)		(A, C♯, E)		
(1, 3, 5, ♭7)		(9, ♭5, 13)		

G7 arpeggio	plus	E major arpeggio	=	G13♭9
(G, B, D, F)		(E, G♯, B)		
(1, 3, 5, ♭7)		(13, ♭9, 3)		

68 E/G7

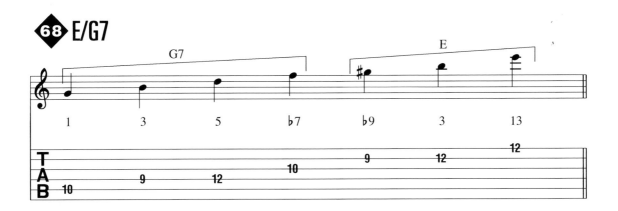

G7				E		
1	3	5	♭7	♭9	3	13

G7 arpeggio	plus	D♭ major arpeggio	=	G7$^{♭9}_{♭5}$
(G, B, D, F)		(D♭, F, A♭)		
(1, 3, 5, ♭7)		(♭5, ♭7, ♭9)		

69 D♭/G7

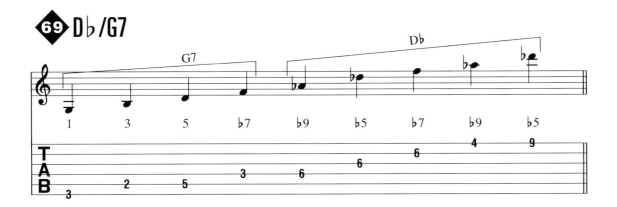

G7				D♭				
1	3	5	♭7	♭9	♭5	♭7	♭9	♭5

70 D♭/G7

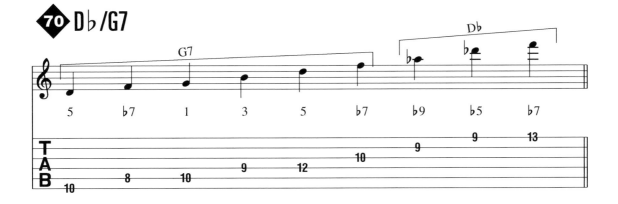

G7						D♭		
5	♭7	1	3	5	♭7	♭9	♭5	♭7

Symmetrical Interval Stacks

This is a process of stacking one particular interval upon itself, then analyzing it to see what chordal sound is created and to which chords it could be applied. For example, stacking minor thirds will create a diminished arpeggio which is commonly used against the dominant chord. Stacking major thirds will create an augmented arpeggio, which is also commonly used against the dominant chord.

INTERVALS STACKED IN 4THS:

For a major 7 chord, start on the 7th and compare the notes. (i.e. for a Cmaj7 chord, start on B.)

(B E A D G C F)
(7 3 6 9 5 1 11)

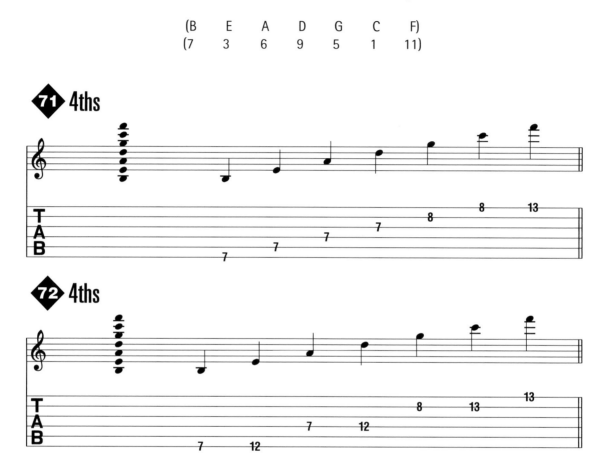

INTERVALS STACKED IN ♭5THS

For a dominant chord, start on the root and compare the notes. (G D♭ G D♭)
(1 ♭5 1 ♭5) etc.

This will work for any chord with a ♭5 in it.

INTERVALS STACKED IN 5THS

For a major 7 chord, start on the root and compare the notes.

(G	D	A	E	B	F#)
(1	5	9	13	3	7)

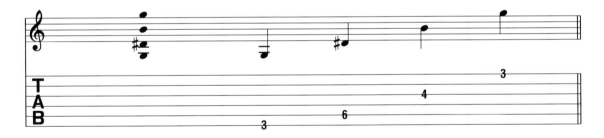

INTERVALS STACKED IN MINOR 6THS

For a dominant chord, start on the root and compare the notes.

(G	D#	B	G)
(1	#5	3	1)	etc.

This will work for any augmented chord.

INTERVALS STACKED IN 6THS

For a dominant chord, start on the ♭7 and compare the notes. (For a G7 chord, start on F.)

(F	D	B	A♭)
(♭7	5	3	♭9)

This will create a G7♭9 sound.

Practice Hints

Try practicing using eighth notes. This should improve your technique and help the music to sound relatively melodic. Regarding the examples below, notice:

1) long ascending and descending melodic lines through chordal changes.

2) the occasional use of common tones to connect the two arpeggios.

3) that an arpeggio may begin not only on its root, but on any of its chord tones.

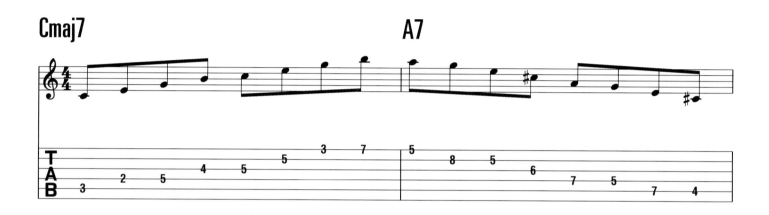

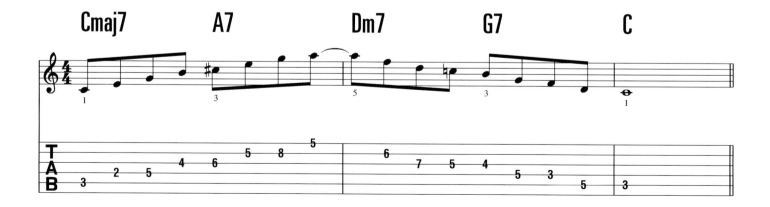

Sequences

Any series of notes may be played in sequences. By taking an arpeggio and numbering its tones (1, 2, 3, 4), we can invent many different interesting sequences. They are very helpful in building technique and lending ideas for improvisation and composition. Try to realize their melodic possibilities instead of just zooming through them for the sake of flashy technique.

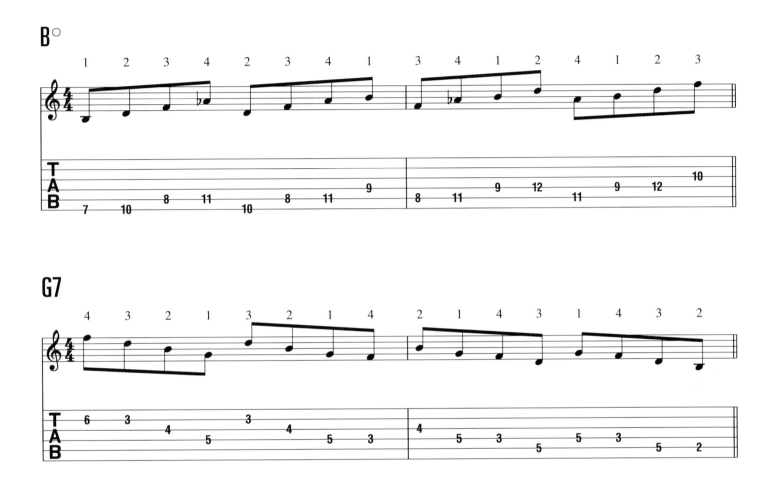

Putting It Together

These are the chord changes of a popular tune utilizing most of the arpeggio principles discussed in this book.

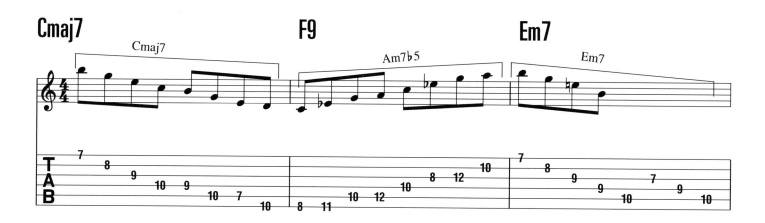

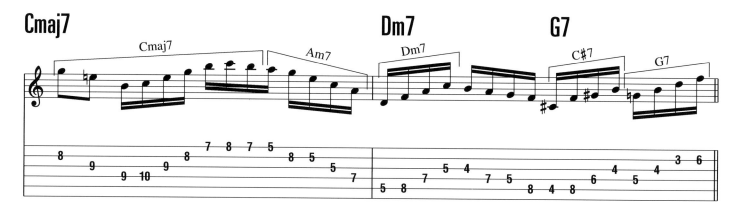

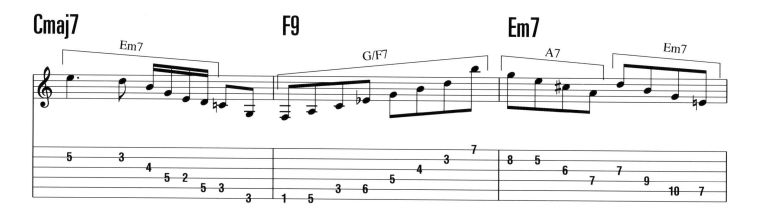

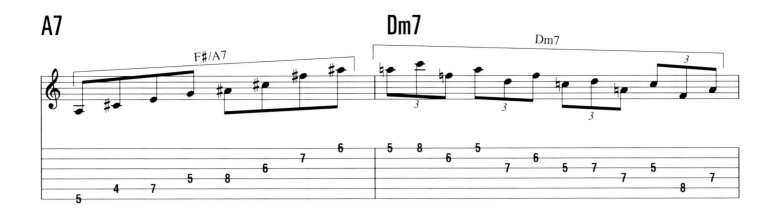

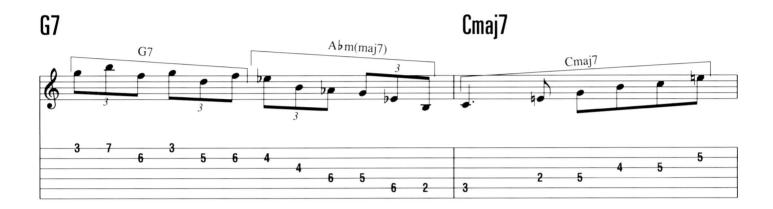

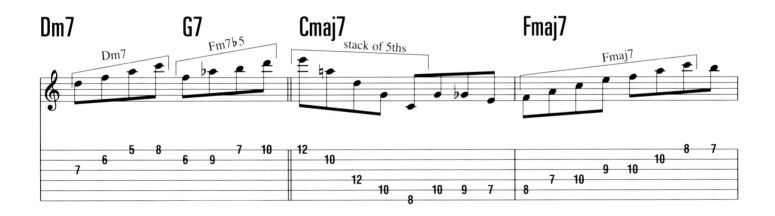

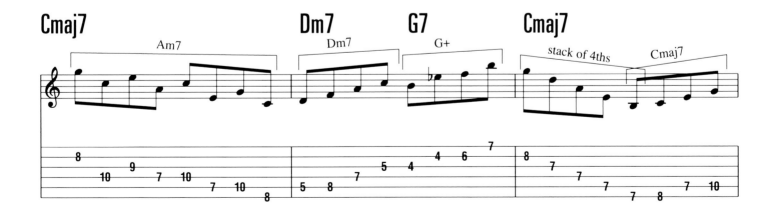

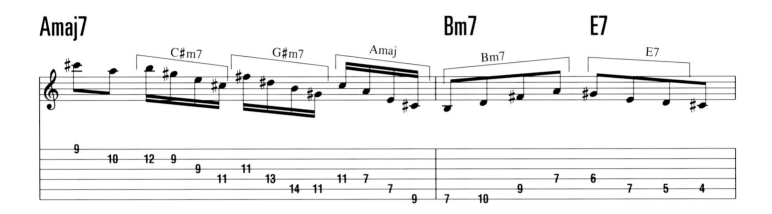

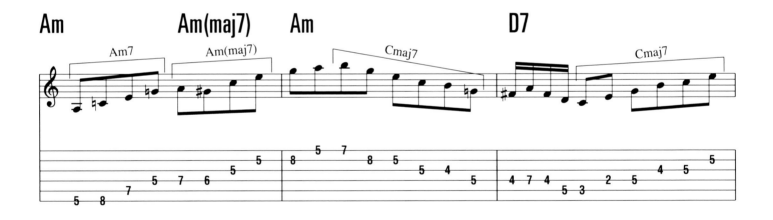

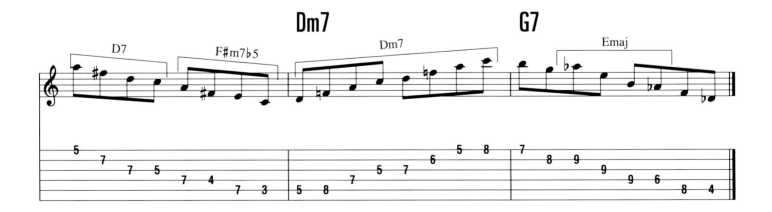